SETTING YOU FREE TO MAKE
RIGHT
CHOICES

LEADERS GUIDE
JR. HIGH/SR. HIGH EDITION

JOSH MCDOWELL

World Bridge Press
Nashville, Tennessee

Reprinted July 1995, December 1995, May 1998

ISBN 0-8054-9829-x

Distributed to the trade by Broadman and Holman Publishers.

Dewey Decimal Classification: 248.83
Subject Heading: DECISION MAKING/CHOICE (PSYCHOLOGY) /YOUTH—RELIGIOUS

Unless otherwise indicated, biblical quotations are from: The Holy Bible, *New International Version,* copyright © 1973, 1978, 1984 by International Bible Society. Used by permission.

Verses marked KJV are taken from the *King James Version* of the Bible.

Verses marked NASB are from the *New American Standard Bible.* Copyright © The Lockman Foundation, 1960, 1962, 1963, 1971, 1972, 1973, 1975, 1977. Used by permission.

Printed in the United States of America

World Bridge Press
127 Ninth Avenue, North
Nashville, Tennessee 37234

Table of Contents

About the Author 4

Introduction 5

Group Session 1 ... It's a Free-for-All 11

Group Session 2 ... God on the Stage 15

Group Session 3 ... Whose Rules Rule? 20

Group Session 4 ... The Four Cs 25

Group Session 5 ... Honest to God 29

Group Session 6 ... What the World Needs Now 33

Group Session 7 ... Sweet Chastity 36

Group Session 8 ... Welcome to the Next Level 40

About the Author

Josh McDowell is an internationally known speaker, author, and traveling representative for Campus Crusade for Christ. A graduate of Wheaton College and Talbot Theological Seminary, he has written more than thirty-five books and appeared in numerous films, videos, and television series. He and his wife, Dottie, live in Dallas, Texas, with their four children.

Introduction
by Josh McDowell

You and I live in challenging times. Our newspapers report it: "Drugs Sold by Children," "Violence Erupts in Classroom," "Crime Takes Over Streets." News magazines document it. "The fraying of America's moral fabric has become a national obsession."[1] "In a new *Newsweek* poll, 76 percent of adults agree that the United States is in moral and spiritual decline."[2] The Christian community fears it: Based on my interaction with the Christian community, "the number one fear among Christian parents (pastors and youth leaders) is they will not be able to pass on their values to the next generation."

In our own 1994 national study conducted among churched youth ages 11-18, it showed that just within the last three months:

- 66% lied to a parent, teacher or another adult
- 59% lied to one of their peers
- 36% cheated on an exam
- 23% intentionally tried to hurt someone

Additionally:

- 55% have engaged in sexual behavior by age 18
- 50% say they're stressed out
- 55% say they're confused

Something fundamentally wrong has happened in our culture that is shaking the very foundation of our society, especially our youth. According to a recent news magazine, 68 percent of Americans are dissatisfied with the way things are going in this country and 80 percent of them believe our problem is the "moral decline of people in general." King David's question is as pertinent today as when he asked it: *"When the foundations are being destroyed, what can the righteous do?"* (Ps. 11:3).

The Right from Wrong Campaign is designed to answer that question. That is why we are collaborating with over 40 denominational and parachurch leaders "to launch a nationwide grassroots effort to resource parents, grandparents, pastors, youth workers, children's workers, and Christian educators to equip youth and children to know right from wrong, enabling them to make right choices."

Our Youth Are Confused About Truth

As we examine our youth's views about morality, it is apparent that the foundations upon which many parents, pastors, and youth leaders attempt to build are crumbling. Traditional biblical concepts are eroding; a Judeo-Christian world view is being undermined. Most of our youth lack the most basic moral perspectives that previous generations took for granted. Our study shows that an alarming 57% of our churched youth cannot state an objective standard of truth even exists.

Only 15% of them disagree with the statement: "What is right for one person in a given situation might not be right for another person who encounters the same situation." In other words, 85% of churched kids are liable to reason, "Just because it's wrong for you doesn't mean it's wrong for me." Their idea of the distinction between right and wrong is fluid, something that is subject to change, something that is relative and personal.

Forty-five percent (45%) of our churched youth could not disagree with the statement, "Everything in life is negotiable." The astounding implication of that statistic is that almost half of our young people are unable or unwilling to recognize that some things in life are nonnegotiable. It's unlikely, of course, that they realize the devastating effects of such a view, but that's part of the whole problem. Many of our youth are struggling with the concept of truth and how they are to apply it to their own life and experience. Our kids are confused about what truth is and who defines it; they are uncertain about what truths are absolute and what makes them absolute. And if this is true of our teenagers, you can be certain our younger children are just as confused. Consequently, they are making conditional decisions, choosing what seems to be in their best interest at the time, without reference to any underlying principles to guide their behavior.

What Is Absolute Truth?

Many of our young people simply do not understand or accept absolute truth—that is, that which is true for all people, for all times, for all places. Absolute truth is truth that is objective, universal, and constant.

We all have established various family rules and guidelines. For example, I have established a curfew with my 13-year-old daughter, specifying what time she should be home after a football game. I have told her, "It is not good to stay out beyond 11:00 p.m." I have set a firm guideline to be followed. If she obeys the curfew, she is right; if she violates it, she is wrong. I want my daughter to consider it a hard and fast rule. And, in most cases she does.

But should we consider that guideline—to be home by 11:00 p.m. after every football game—an absolute truth? No. It is not applicable to all people, at all times, in all places. Communities, states, and governments may create various ordinances, regulations, and laws that are to be obeyed, but they are not necessarily absolutes. Ordinances change, regulations expire, and some laws only apply in certain states. In fact, even the curfew rule for my daughter may change someday. An absolute truth, on the other hand, is objective, universal, and constant.

If our youth are going to learn how to determine right from wrong, they must know what truths are absolute and why. They need to know what standards of behavior are right for all people, for all times, for all places. They need to know who determines truth—and why.

Why Truth Matters

You may say, "Come on, Josh, all this talk about absolutes seems so abstract. Do you really think that a young person's views about truth will really make a difference in their behavior?" That is one of the astounding insights of this research. The study indicates that when our youth do not accept an objective standard of truth they become:

- 36% more likely to lie to you as a parent!
- 48% more likely to cheat on an exam!
- 2 times more likely to try to physically hurt someone!
- 2 times more likely to watch a pornographic film!
- 2 $1/4$ times more likely to steal!
- 3 times more likely to use illegal drugs!
- 6 times more likely to attempt suicide!

If our youth fail to embrace truth as an objective standard that governs their lives, the study shows it will make them:

- 65% more likely to mistrust people!
- 2 times more likely to be disappointed!
- 2 times more likely to be angry with life!
- 2 times more likely to be resentful!

How our youth think about truth has a definite affect on their behavior—the choices they make, and the attitudes they adopt.

There Is Hope

It's a frightening prospect to raise our children in the midst of a "perverse and crooked generation." There are no easy answers, but there is hope. It is not too late to reinforce the crumbling foundations. If you and I are willing to set aside the "quick fix" mentality and face the stark reality of what we as a Christian community have allowed (and perhaps unwittingly adopted ourselves), I believe there is hope.

First, I suggest you as the group leader obtain and read the book *Right from Wrong—What You Need to Know to Help Youth Make Right Choices*. As a truth apologetic it will provide you with a solid defense of truth. It is also the text upon which this entire *Setting You Free to Make Right Choices Workbook* for youth is based. Another resource I suggest your church utilize is the *Setting Youth Free to Make Right Choices* Video Series.

The *Setting You Free to Make Right Choices Workbook* is designed as an 8-week program and the *Setting Youth Free to Make Right Choices* Video Series is created as a 5-week program. Combined together, they make for an entire quarter for your youth group. Your church can begin this Right from Wrong emphasis by starting first with either the Video Series or the Workbooks, depending on your approach.

The Video Series is highly motivational and will challenge your entire youth group, fun seekers included, to embrace the concept that right moral choices must be based on an absolute standard of right and wrong. The series builds a powerful defense for truth. It includes compelling video and film dramatic vignettes, music videos, teaching sessions, a Leader's Guide with creative group activities, and the companion book entitled *Truth Slayers—The Battle of Right from Wrong.* The entire Video Series teaches your youth how to determine right from wrong and motivates them to apply the Right from Wrong message to their lives. The entire group is now primed to begin the *Setting You Free to Make Right Choices Workbook* 8-session study.

But because the Video Series is highly motivational, challenging, and leads up to the Workbook does not mean you cannot start by first using the Workbooks. The *Setting You Free to Make Right Choices Workbook* empowers students with a making right choices process and calls for practicing it out in their everyday lives. This course requires a higher degree of spiritual interest and commitment by your students than does the Video Series in that the Workbooks call for 20-25 minutes of daily exercises to be completed between group sessions. However, at the end of this course students will be highly motivated to share this habit-forming method of making right choices with their friends. The group will be primed to invite their non-churched friends to the Video Series as a youth group outreach.

The "Right from Wrong" Video Series and Workbook resources are like two circular tracks that form a figure eight. (See Diagram A.)

Diagram A

Your approach may be to first begin with a smaller, but committed, group of students with the Workbooks and then use your newly motivated group to conduct a Video Series outreach. Or, you may elect to begin with your entire youth group participating in the Video Series, using it to motivate the whole group to begin the Workbooks. Regardless of which track you enter first, both experiences compliment each other, yet stand independent of the other.

There are other Right from Wrong workbooks and videos directed to other age groups. There is a 5-part Video Series and an 8-week Workbook directed to adults entitled *Truth Matters for You and Tomorrow's Generation.* There is an 8-week Workbook for college students called, *Out of the Moral Maze,* and two Workbooks—one directed to younger children (grades 1-3) and one to older children (grades 4-6) entitled, *Truth Works— Making Right Choices.*

Meet with your pastor or church staff to discuss initiating a churchwide emphasis on Right from Wrong. Such an emphasis directed to each age group of the church can become a powerful tool to help rebuild and strengthen the foundations of truth. (More information on resources to help you launch such a churchwide campaign is found on p. 45.)

Setting You Free to Make Right Choices Workbook

As the youth group leader you will be helping your students discover a simple four-step process for making the right choices related to issues about honesty, sexual purity, and love. The four steps are the Steps of Truth. We call them the "4Cs" process of making right choices.

Consider the choice
Compare our attitudes and actions to God
Commit to God's ways
Count on God's protection and provision

This four-step process to making right choices will create a new way of thinking and acting as a student learns how choices based on God and His Word is always the right choice. Following is the process you will be teaching:

1. Consider the Choice

When faced with a moral choice we want our youth to first stop to consider what determines its rightness or wrongness.

The culture has conditioned many to believe each individual has the right to determine for themselves what is right and wrong. Truth, in this view, is subjective and personal and there is no absolute right and wrong that governs a person's life. In other words, it's up to the individual to determine the rightness and wrongness of their own attitudes or actions.

The Steps of Truth is a new way to process our moral choices. And in this first step we must ask: **"Who determines what is right or wrong in this situation?"** This step erects a STOP sign of sorts to alert our young people that their attitudes and actions are judged by someone other than themselves and they are not to justify their behavior based on their own selfish interests.

2. Compare It to God

This next step answers the question: **"Who determines what is right or wrong absolutely?"** Here we want students to acknowledge there is an absolute righteous God and that they must compare their attitudes and actions to Him and His words to determine whether they are right or wrong.

This step points them to the revelation of Jehovah God in His written Word. His Word (Old and New Testament Scripture) gives all of us specific and absolute guidelines as to the rightness or wrongness of attitudes and actions. But these guidelines are not simply the "do's and don'ts" of the law, they are a reflection of the very nature and character of God Himself.

3. Commit to God's Way

This third step is where the "rubber meets the road"—**this is decision time.** Considering the choice and comparing it to God are necessary steps to show us that our ways are not like God's ways. It shows us that our tendency is to justify, rationalize, and excuse ourselves, all in an attempt to legitimize our selfish interests and pleasures. When we compare our attitudes and actions to God as God, we ADMIT that His character and nature defines right and wrong absolutely. Those attitudes and actions that are like Him are considered right, and those attitudes and actions that are not like Him are considered wrong.

But when we commit to God's way it means we turn from our selfishness and those attitudes and actions in question that are unlike Him and SUBMIT to Him as Lord of our lives and rely on His power to live out His way in us.

4. Count on God's Protection and Provision

When we humbly ADMIT God's sovereignty and sincerely SUBMIT to His loving authority, we can not only begin to see clearly the distinctions between right and wrong, but we can also count on God's protection and provision. Here in this fourth step **we want our youth to thank God for His loving protection and provision.** This doesn't mean everything will be rosy, in fact, God says that we may suffer for righteousness sake. But such suffering has great rewards. Living according to God's way and allowing the Holy Spirit to live through us brings many spiritual blessings, like freedom from guilt, a clear conscience, the joy of sharing Christ, and most importantly the love and smile of God in our lives.

Additionally, we enjoy many physical, emotional, psychological, and relational benefits when we are obedient to God. While God's protection and provision should not be our primary motivation to obey God, it certainly provides a powerful reinforcement for us to choose the right and reject the wrong.

The purpose of the *Setting You Free to Make*

Right Choices Workbook is:

- To teach students what truths are absolute and why

- To teach students a model for making right moral choices through the 4Cs process

- To provide opportunity for youth to practice making right choices so it becomes a habit

- To provide students with a support group atmosphere of encouragement, accountability, and prayer

Students need to know that God truly cares about the choices they make. *"For I know the plans I have for you," declares the Lord, "plans to prosper you and not to harm you, plans to give you hope and a future" (Jer. 29:11).* Ultimately, making right moral choices based upon God and His Word as our standard of right and wrong comes down to trusting God. Do we really believe God has a plan to prosper us? If He does, and I assure you He does, then living in relationship with Him is not only right, it is in our long-term best interest.

This program will enable you to lead students to discover that a personal relationship with God is fundamental in making right moral choices in life. You play a vital role in helping them nurture this fresh understanding of their relationship to God as it relates to right choices. Together, with God's help, we can strengthen the moral foundations of our young people and provide them with clear direction on how to always make right moral choices.

How to Use This Material

The *Setting You Free to Make Right Choices Leader's Guide* is one part of an inductive, interactive learning system. It is designed to be used with the *Setting You Free to Make Right Choices Student Workbook.* The Leader's Guide will help you prepare for and conduct weekly group sessions; the Student Workbook is intended for individual use by each student.

Each session plan consists of the following:

- **Session Aims** A concise two- or three-point statement of the session's focus.

- **Before the Session** A checklist of things to do in preparation for the group meeting.

- **Session Overview** A quick look at the components of each 60-minute session.

- **Theme Verse** A Bible verse that reflects the theme of the meeting.

- **Warm-Up** An active, fun-filled introduction to the session.

- **Look Back** A period of reflection and discussion about the significance of the Warm-Up period or the previous week's Workbook studies. Review memory verses.

- **Work Out** A time in which students discuss and experience the main teaching of the session.

- **Word Up** Scripture study with questions to guide discussion.

- **Wrap Up** A short wrap-up to conclude the session.

- **Plan Ahead** A few quick notes to allow the leader to make preparation for the next session.

Each session is designed to be ready-to-use with a minimum amount of preparation. However, the group leader should give careful and thorough attention to the "Before the Session" checklist, which include reminders to pray for the students and the sessions.

The group sessions are designed to clarify and reinforce the concepts covered in the *Right Choices Student Workbook.* Every student participating in the group sessions should be provided his or her own Student Workbook to take home for daily use. The leader should strongly encourage and frequently remind students to complete the daily studies that lead students in the discovery of truth (in a manner and to an extent that the group sessions cannot duplicate or replace).

Tips for Encouraging Healthy Group Discussion

Junior high and high school students love to talk. They like to be asked about their opinions, they enjoy expressing their own ideas, and they will often talk—even in front of their parents and peers—if they believe someone else is truly interested in what they have to say.

For that reason, this *Right Choices Leader's Guide* contains many suggested questions to encourage discussion. Leading a healthy group discussion requires more than simply asking good questions, however. The following tips can help make any group of teens into a lively, thinking, talking group.

1. Don't be afraid of silence. Many teachers and group leaders make the mistake of asking a thought-provoking question and then, when no one answers immediately, moving on too quickly to the next question. The wise leader will try to create an atmosphere in which careful thought is encouraged—by the wise use of silence. Allow a brief time for thought after each question if necessary, then signal for someone to speak up by simply asking, "Anybody?" or "Someone finish your thought out loud."

2. Let discussion follow its own path (without letting the group stray too far). Don't be in a hurry to move to the next question in your Leader's Guide. But be careful not to let your students get off on tangents not related to the topic of discussion.

3. As often as possible, follow a comment with another question. After a student has made an observation, ask "Can you think of an example?" or ask how the rest of the group responds.

4. Don't feel obligated to ask all (or exclusively) the questions in the Leader's Guide. If your group's time is limited, highlight the questions you wish to ask. Add questions suited to your own group as discussion develops.

5. Encourage students to talk. Begin questions with phrases like, "What do you think about..." or "How do you react to...?" or "Would you do that differently?" Such phrases avoid giving the impression that you're looking for some "right" answer. You need not allow error to go unchallenged; just be careful to offer corrections in a way that will encourage that student to speak up again. (If a student makes a comment that you cannot allow to go unchallenged, encourage gentle correction by asking, "Does anyone agree or disagree with that statement?" or temper your correction by saying something like, "You bring up an important point, Brad, but we need to remember that...").

6. When it's practical, "prime the pump" of discussion by planting questions or "sniping" at the most vocal, well-spoken students. If your group is slow to start discussions, jot one or two questions onto index cards and give them to some of your most outgoing students before the session, asking them to be ready to offer comments if others don't jump in quickly. You may also ask several confident youth if they will allow you to call them by name to answer a question if the discussion begins to lag.

7. Finally, refer frequently to lucid observations students have made. "Remember what Janice said?..." "A few minutes ago, Guy made the point that..." Such references not only remind students that you listen to them; it boosts the impression that they have something important to contribute. The more you use what *they* say to make a point, the more points they will be anxious to make.

[1] Howard Fineman, "The Virtuecrats," *Newsweek,* 13 June 1994, 3.

[2] Ibid., 31.

group session 1

It's a Free-for-All

SESSION AIMS

This session will:

- introduce the students to the format of the *Right Choices* study
- bring students to realize the danger and devastation of everyone "doing what is right in his or her own eyes"
- prompt students to recognize their need of a standard for moral decisions

BEFORE THE SESSION

☐ Review the learning activities for the coming week in the *Right Choices Student Workbook*.

☐ Read through the Session Plan. Feel free to adjust the activities according to your group's needs. Highlight portions you consider especially difficult or important for easy reference during the session. Make notes to help personalize the Session Plan.

☐ Pray for your students. Ask God to help you accomplish the aims of the upcoming session, and to motivate and guide students as they pursue the daily sessions in the Student Workbook.

☐ Inflate 50 balloons of two colors (for example, 25 blue balloons and 25 white balloons). Separate according to color. They will be used in the Warm-Up activity.

☐ Have a chalkboard and chalk or newsprint and marker available for the session.

☐ Photocopy Reproducible Handout 1A ("Tough Calls") for the group, and obtain a pencil or pen for every student.

☐ Acquire a *King James Version* of the Bible and a *New International Version* for use during the session.

☐ Ask a student before the group session begins to be prepared to close in prayer.

☐ Photocopy the skit, "The Robbery" page 18, for

two or three volunteers (depending on the size of your group) to take home with them in preparation for group session 2.

SESSION OVERVIEW

- Warm-Up (10-15 min.)
- Look Back (15 min.)
- Word Up (10 min.)
- Work Out (20 min.)
- Plan Ahead (after the session)

THEME VERSE: In those days there was no king in Israel: every man did that which was right in his own eyes (Judg. 21:25, KJV).

SESSION PLAN

WARM-UP (10-15 minutes)

Try to begin the Warm-Up activity approximately 5 minutes before your typical meeting starting time. Divide all students who are present into two teams. Line each team facing the other on opposite sides of an open area at the front of the room (clear as much space as possible). Create a line of 10 balloons (separated by color) on the floor behind each team (for example, one team will have all blue balloons and the other team will have all white).

Explain that each team has 10 balloons, all of the same color, on the floor at their end of the room. The purpose of the game is to capture the opposing team's balloons (each worth two points) without losing your own balloons (each worth one point). Only inflated balloons will be counted for points. Team members must keep their hands in their pockets or behind their backs. Balloons may be kicked, blown, etc., but may not be picked up by hand. The first team to possess 20 points wins. As new students enter, guide them to join one of two teams playing the game.

If the first game has not ended after five minutes, suspend play, total points, and declare a winning team. Replenish the balloons and begin a new game, explaining that the object is the same, but *that there are no rules*—each team may play by its own rules (for example, a team may decide to intentionally burst all its balloons to prevent the other team from winning). If neither team has won after three minutes, end the game and instruct students to be seated.

LOOK BACK (20-25 minutes)

Ask: **Which game did you think was more fun? Why?** Allow time for students to respond. Have youth share how they felt when they were playing the game with no rules.

Tell students, **Those games we just played are a lot like the world. Sometimes it seems like the rules that everybody once played by have disappeared. Sometimes it seems like no one is playing by the rules anymore.**

Ask: **Do you agree or disagree? Why?** Give opportunity for students to give examples of ways in which people no longer "play by the rules." Some possibilities:

- it's "cool" to carry a gun or knife

- it's "right" to sleep with someone you love, even if you're not married

- it's "okay" to have babies outside of marriage

- it's "no big deal" to copy homework or cheat on a test.

Ask: **Have you ever heard someone justify some behavior that you thought was obviously wrong?** Encourage students to share several examples, then ask, **Why couldn't the other people see that they were doing something wrong?** Allow ample time for students to offer suggestions.

Say: **You're not alone if you feel that most people are no longer playing by the rules. Many people don't even recognize what the rules are anymore. Our society has come to a point where even the "experts" can't agree on what's right and what's wrong. It has become a free-for-all,** and, **like our balloon game, that can create a lot of confusion and frustration. But how do we solve it? What can we do?**

WORD UP (5-10 minutes)

Ask two students to copy *Judges 21:25* from the Bible (one from the KJV and one from the NIV) onto a chalkboard or newsprint, and ask the group to read it in unison aloud.

Ask: **Those words were written thousands of years ago about the Israelites during the time of the judges. Do you know anything about that period of Israel's history?** (It was a time of unrest, the days of Deborah, and Gideon, and Samson.)

Ask a student to read *Judges 2:11-19* while two other students record on the chalkboard (or newsprint) the words or phrases from the reading that describe those days of Israel's history. Take a few moments to review the list on the chalkboard.

Ask: **What was wrong with everyone doing as he (or she) saw fit?** Allow answers from several students, but try to guide them to express the dangers of "everyone doing that which is right in his own eyes," much as we see happening around us today.

Ask: **How else are we supposed to live, if not according to what we think is right?** Try to guide students to express our need for a standard in deciding right and wrong.

WORK OUT (25-30 minutes)

Say: **To help us answer those questions, we're going to take a little quiz, called "Tough Calls."** Pass out pencils and copies of Handout 1A ("Tough Calls") to the students. Instruct the students to complete the quiz according to the instructions at the top.

When the students have completed the quiz, allow them to take turns reading a question and reporting their answers. Have fun with the quiz, and let them have fun with it. Invite them to come up with other, more creative answers of their own. Before moving on to the next question, of course, ask which answer makes the most sense and would produce a solution, and invite students to discuss why that is so. Emphasize, in each case, the need for a standard, the necessity of a source that is dependable and original.

After all the answers have been reviewed, ask: **What did each of those situations have in common? What was necessary in each case?** The answer, of course, is a "standard," something (measuring cup, rule book, etc.) that could supply a definite, authoritative answer.

WRAP UP (5 minutes)

Say: **Our world today—our schools, our government, our media, our society—is a lot like Israel during the time of the judges. It's a free-for-all, in which everyone does what he or she thinks is right.**

But just as we need a measuring cup to make a good birthday cake or a rule book to make a regulation baseball field, we need a standard of some kind in order to make decisions of right and wrong.

State: **It's obvious that if you need to measure a cup of milk, you look for a measuring cup. It's obvious that if you need to measure a distance of miles, you need an odometer. . .** Ask: **But what kind of standard can we look to when we have questions about right and wrong?** Allow students to offer suggestions, and engage in discussion with the leader and with each other, without specifying for them the answer to your question.

Say: **This week in our *Right Choices* Workbooks, you'll begin to discover the danger of living in a free-for-all society, the need for a standard, and just what that standard is.**

Ask for any final comments about today's lesson.

Ask a student to close this week's session in prayer.

PLAN AHEAD (after close of session)

Distribute student Workbooks.

Enlist two or three students to practice and participate in the skit, "The Robbery."

List student names, addresses, and telephone numbers here for easy reference.

Answer the following questions, circling the best answer.

1. You and a friend have a disagreement. You say the distance from your house to school is about three miles; your friend insists it's at least four miles. What do you do?

(a) order a pizza and forget about the whole thing

(b) jump into your car and measure the distance on the odometer

(c) lock your friend in a closet until he or she admits you were right

2. You decide to bake a surprise birthday cake for your mom. The recipe calls for one-and-one-third cups of milk. You:

(a) skip that part of the recipe

(b) pour milk straight from the bottle, guessing the right amount

(c) use a measuring cup

3. Your algebra teacher marked your test answer wrong, but gave the rest of the class credit for the same answer. You:

(a) politely ask the teacher to double-check your answer against the key

(b) decide never to speak to that teacher again

(c) decide to beat up everyone in the class

4. You and a friend are helping the baseball coach build a new baseball diamond. Your friend asks you how far apart the bases are supposed to be from each other. You don't know, but you:

(a) pick a spot in the field and announce, "this feels about right"

(b) look up the dimensions of a regulation field in the rule book

(c) offer to flip a coin (heads, you decide; tails, he decides)

5. You and a friend are writing a story together, and neither of you can remember how to spell, *macroglobulinemia.* You:

(a) give it your best shot and hope it's close

(b) find a new friend (one who can spell)

(c) look it up in the dictionary

6. You finish your math homework in class, but Mr. Scrubneck says you're allowed to check your answers. You:

(a) place a large ✔ beside each problem

(b) compare your answers to the answers given in the back of the book

(c) hold your homework paper at arm's length, and say, "Yeah, they look right to me"

SCORE YOURSELF: Add the following number of points for each letter answer you gave:

(1) a-1 b-2 c-0   (2) a-0 b-1 c-2

(3) a-2 b-1 c-0   (4) a-1 b-2 c-0

(5) a-0 b-0 c-2   (6) a-0 b-2 c-0

If you scored 10-12 points: Nice job. You obviously weren't born yesterday.

If you scored 6-9 points: Well, you might have been born yesterday, but you've certainly grown since then!

If you scored 0-5 points: Judging from your answers, you were born this morning. Happy Birthday!

group session 2

God On the Stage

Session Aims

This session will:

- reinforce the contents of the Week One Workbook studies

- introduce students to the concept that we must "learn God's ways" in order to know Him (His nature and character), and we must know Him before we can compare our actions to Him

- prepare for Week Two Workbook studies, in which students will be introduced to the "test of truth" process (of precept-principle-person) and will begin to practice the process

BEFORE THE SESSION

❏ Review the learning activities for the coming week in the *Right Choices* Workbook.

❏ Read through the Session Plan, adjusting portions as needed, highlighting things you wish to emphasize, and making notes to personalize the Session Plan.

❏ Call the students who will be participating in the skit to remind them to arrive early and offer any last-minute support that may be necessary.

❏ Pray for your students. Ask God to help you accomplish the aims of the upcoming session, and to motivate and guide students as they pursue the daily sessions in the *Right Choices* Workbook.

❏ Photocopy a copy of Reproducible Handout 2A ("Teach Me Your Ways") for each student to use during the session.

❏ Have a chalkboard and chalk or newsprint and markers available for the session.

❏ Ask a student (before the group session begins) to be prepared to close in prayer.

❏ Memorize the "This Week's Verse," memory Scripture for Week 1.

SESSION OVERVIEW
- Warm-Up (5-10 min.)
- Look Back (20-25 min.)
- Word Up (15 min.)
- Work Out (5 min.)
- Wrap Up (5 min.)
- Plan Ahead (after the session)

THEME VERSE: He is the Rock. . . a God of truth and without iniquity, just and right is he (Deut. 32:4, KJV).

SESSION PLAN

WARM-UP (5—10 minutes)
Welcome your students.

Enlist a student to open today's session in prayer. Introduce the skit, "The Robbery."

Have students perform the skit, "The Robbery" (see Reproducible Session Activity, page 18).

Allow time for students to repeat the memory Scripture verse from memory. Encourage students to learn the verse if they have not done so.

LOOK BACK (20-25 minutes)
Thank skit participants and allow a moment for them to join the rest of the group.

Ask: **Who do you think was right, the clerk or the robber? Or neither?** Allow as many students as possible to respond, then ask, **Why?**

Ask: **What point do you think that skit makes?** Allow students to offer answers without correction or comment.

Ask: **Did either the clerk or the robber appeal to any objective, universal, or constant standard of truth?** The answer, of course, is no; guide students to express, if possible, that their argument went nowhere because neither of them referred to God, the only objective, universal, or constant standard of truth.

Ask: **What should have been the clerk's answer when the robber asked, "Says who?" Why?**

15

Ask for two volunteers to act out (in an unscripted role play) how they think the conversation might have gone if the clerk had answered "God," when the robber asked, "Says who?" Urge them to be as realistic as possible (and be prepared to discuss the result). If time permits, ask: **Could the conversation possibly have ended in a different way? How?** Allow another pair of students to perform a role play, adding their own ending.

Say: **Whether the robber is willing to admit it or not, we discovered this week in our** *Right Choices* **Workbooks that God is the only True Standard of right and wrong. Nothing else will fill the bill. . .**

- **individual opinions won't do, because they are so often dictated by fickle feelings and faulty thinking;**

- **cultural norms aren't reliable, because they often change with the scenery;**

- **civil law isn't sufficient, because it is subject to change with time.**

Only God is objective, universal, and constant. He is the God of truth.

WORD UP (15–20 minutes)

Ask students to open their Workbooks to page 18. Ask, **What three words did you put in the blanks?** After they answer (objective, universal, constant) have students turn to page 22 and discuss their answers to the last three statements.

Say: **Once we realize, however, that God is the standard we need, how do we apply the moral choices we face—whether to lie, or steal, or cheat, for example—to the Standard? How do we know whether any of the choices we face measure up to the Standard? How do we know whether something is like God or not?** Allow students to respond.

Divide the group into smaller groups of two or three. Distribute Reproducible Handout 2A ("Teach Me Your Ways") to each student and ask them to complete the handout together, and then to be prepared to report back to the entire group when they're finished.

Call group back together after 10 minutes, and ask each group to share their answer to each question in turn. Emphasize to the students that this is a "discovery" exercise, so they do not need to feel any pressure to give the "right" answer or embarrassment if another group's answer differs from their own. The purpose is to discover together how we can begin referring our choices to God, who is the Standard.

WORK OUT (5 minutes)

Instruct youth to turn to *Hebrews 1:1* and call on someone to read the verse. After a student reads those brief verses remind youth that God has not left us to guess whether certain things are right or wrong. He has spoken. He spoke through prophets in the Old Testament times and through Jesus in New Testament times. Ask, **How does God speak today?** Allow students to answer; draw from them the realization that one way God speaks today is through His Word.

Enlist one of the students to write the statement, "God has revealed Himself through His Word" on the chalkboard or on a sheet of newsprint.

Ask: **Why is it important that God reveals Himself to us through His Word?** Allow students to offer suggestions or answers before going on. After allowing a few moments for student contribution, say: **Because He has revealed Himself through His Word, we can know Him—the God who is the only standard of right and wrong—by learning His ways. How is it that we learn His ways?** Prompt students to recall their answers from the Handout.

WRAP UP (5 minutes)

Say: **In order to make any judgment about right or wrong we must bring God onto the stage. Without Him, any assertions about the wrongness of murder, rape, bigotry, or hatred are nothing more than just human opinion. Such an opinion is not objective, it is not universal, and it is not constant. But God is all of those things.**

Share with the students that this week in our *Right Choices* Workbooks, we'll discover a process for learning God's ways, a technique by which we can determine the rightness or wrongness of basic moral choices by comparing those choices to the standard we need—God Himself.

Ask the students if they have any final questions

or comments before the closing prayer. Take a few prayer requests and allow students to close this week's session with a series of short sentence prayers, after which you will conclude with a final word of prayer.

PLAN AHEAD (after close of session)

Evaluate today's group session and ask yourself these questions:

- What other resources did I need that would have made this session better?

- Are the students understanding the connection with the *Right Choices* Workbook and the group sessions?

- Am I beginning and ending on time? Am I covering all that I need to cover to make this a meaningful time for the students?

Prepare to call the members of the group and encourage them to stay current in their *Right Choices* Workbook and thank them for the contribution they are making to the group sessions. Ask if there is anything you can pray specifically for them.

Record date called, the member's name, and specific prayer requests for each group member.

Reproducible Session Activity

The Robbery
A Play in One Act

CAST:
Clerk [male or female]
Police Officer [male or female]
Robber [male or female]

PROPS:
Table
Paper money
Long coat
  [trench coat or
  duster]

[Clerk stands behind a table like a store clerk. Robber enters in a long coat with his or her hands thrust into the pockets]

CLERK: May I help you?

ROBBER: *[pointing at Clerk through the pocket of the coat as if concealing a gun]* Yeah, give me all your money. And make it fast!

CLERK: *[pathetically]* But this is Christmas Eve. And this is the orphanage gift shop.

ROBBER: Just give me the money, okay?

CLERK: You don't want to do this.

ROBBER: I don't? Why not?

CLERK: Because it's wrong.

ROBBER: Maybe it's wrong for you, but it ain't wrong for me.

CLERK: Yes it is.

ROBBER: No it's not.

[Clerk and Robber repeat— Yes it is. No it's not.— argumentatively several times]

CLERK: But stealing is wrong!

ROBBER: Says who?

CLERK: Everybody! Everybody knows that.

ROBBER: I don't.

CLERK: Well you're wrong then!

ROBBER: Says who?

CLERK: Not this again.

ROBBER: Look, you keep saying stealing is wrong. Maybe it is—for you. But you can't tell me what's right or wrong for me. So give me all your money.

CLERK: But the law says it's wrong.

ROBBER: The law can change; the law once said it was wrong for women and minorities to vote. So give me all your money or I may have to shoot you.

CLERK: That would be wrong, too.

ROBBER: Says who?

CLERK: Here we go again.

[Suddenly, Police Officer bursts onto the scene and surprises the Robber; a brief confrontation ensues, and the Officer arrests the Robber]

ROBBER: *[looking at Clerk with hurt look]* You set off some kind of alarm, didn't you?

CLERK: *[smiling proudly]* Yup, sure did.

ROBBER: *[shaking head]* I can't believe it. *[looks at Clerk admonishingly]* That's wrong.

CLERK: *[still smiling]* Says who?

Reproducible Handout 2A

Teach Me Your Ways

Look up *Exodus 33:13,* Moses' request to God after receiving the Law. Write the verse on the lines below:

_____

_____

_____

_____

_____

_____

_____

_____

_____

Have someone in your small group read the verse aloud. Then answer the following questions:

• Moses' words reveal that he had two goals. What were they?

1.

_____

_____

_____

2.

_____

_____

_____

• What did he want God to do to help him achieve those goals?

_____

_____

_____

_____

_____

_____

_____

_____

_____

_____

• What do you think Moses means when he says, "teach me your ways"?

_____

_____

_____

_____

_____

_____

_____

_____

_____

_____

• How could learning God's ways help Moses to know God and find favor with Him?

_____

_____

_____

_____

_____

_____

_____

_____

_____

_____

• How could learning God's ways help us distinguish and defend right from wrong?

_____

_____

_____

_____

_____

_____

_____

group session 3

Whose Rules Rule?

SESSION AIMS

This session will:

- reinforce students' understanding of God's loving motivation (to provide and protect)

- prompt students to the realization that we should make right choices not because they benefit us (though they often do) but because of who God is

- invite students to submit their wills (and their "right" to decide right and wrong) to God (and His revelation of right and wrong)

BEFORE THE SESSION

❑ Review the learning activities for the coming week in the *Right Choices* Workbook.

❑ Read through the Session Plan, adjusting the activities according to your group's size and personality, highlighting portions you consider especially difficult or important, and making notes to personalize the Session Plan.

❑ Pray for your students. Ask God to help you accomplish the aims of the upcoming session, and to motivate and guide students as they pursue the daily sessions in the *Right Choices* Workbook.

❑ Photocopy Reproducible Handout 3A ("The Ten Commandments") on page 24 (two copies for small groups, more for larger groups). You may want to use colorful card stock. Cut around each card to make a set of 10 (one set of Commandments for each small group). Make sure the sets are shuffled well so the Commandments are not in order.

❑ Be sure you have a watch or clock with a second hand available for use during the session.

❑ Prepare three-foot lengths of ribbon, pens or colored felt-tip markers, and bottles of glue (one ribbon and one bottle of glue for each small

group participating in the Ten Commandments Warm-Up and Look Back activities).

❑ Ask a student before the group session begins to be prepared to close in prayer.

❑ Memorize "This Week's Verse," memory Scripture for Week 2.

SESSION OVERVIEW

- Warm-Up (5-10 min.)
- Look Back (20 min.)
- Work Out (10 min.)
- Word Up (15 min.)
- Wrap Up (5 min.)
- Plan Ahead (after the session)

THEME VERSE: "How great you are, O Sovereign Lord! There is no one like you, and there is no God but you" (2 Sam. 7:22).

SESSION PLAN

WARM-UP (5-10 minutes)

Welcome your students and enlist a student to open today's session in prayer.

Divide the students into small groups of three or four. Give each group a complete set of the "Ten Commandments" slips of paper (from Reproducible Handout 3A). Instruct them to place the slips of paper face down on a table or the floor and wait for your signal to begin the game. Inform them that each slip of paper contains one of the Ten Commandments, but that they are out of order, and each group is to work together to sort them into the correct order—in one minute. When each group is ready, give them the signal and begin timing them. After 60 seconds, stop both groups and tell them the order they have now must remain unchanged. Have the groups in turn reveal the results, and compare them silently against the correct order:

1. You shall have no other gods before Me.

2. You shall not make for yourself an idol in the form of anything in heaven above or on the earth beneath or in the waters below.

3. You shall not misuse the name of the Lord your God, for the Lord will not hold anyone guiltless who misuses His name.

4. Remember the Sabbath day by keeping it holy.

5. Honor your father and your mother, so that you may live long in the land the Lord your God is giving you.

6. You shall not murder.

7. You shall not commit adultery.

8. You shall not steal.

9. You shall not give false testimony against your neighbor.

10. You shall not covet your neighbor's house. You shall not covet your neighbor's wife, or his manservant or maidservant, his ox or donkey, or anything that belongs to your neighbor.

Congratulate the group(s) that got all or most of the Commandments in the correct order. Tell students to order their set of Commandments correctly now, and to stay in their groups for the next activity.

Allow students to practice and repeat "This Week's Verse" memory Scripture verses. Encourage students to learn the verse for Session 3.

LOOK BACK (20 minutes)

Say: **Don't feel too bad if you couldn't remember whether "You shall not murder" was number six or seven; some polls show that few people today can list more than a couple of the Ten Commandments. But we're not only going to consider what God's precepts say, we will spend the next few minutes thinking about how they protect and provide for us.**

Remind the students that during this past week their *Right Choices* Workbooks focused on the fact that people who make right choices enjoy the benefits of God's protection and provision... because God said way back in Old Testament times, that His commandments were given for our good, to prosper us and not to harm us. Every precept of God is intended:

1. To reflect His nature and character, and

2. To protect us and provide for us.

Distribute pens or markers to each group. Instruct the students to spend some time brainstorming in their groups about how each Commandment protects us or provides for us. Then have the students write boldly and neatly on each card one or more ways in which that specific Commandment protects us or provides for us (if you have two groups, you may consider assigning one group to list examples of God's provision and the other group to list examples of God's protection). Give them 60 seconds for each Commandment. Get them started and time them. After 60 seconds move them on to Commandment 2 and on down the line until they have completed all Ten Commandments. After 10 minutes, they should have identified 10 ways that those particular precepts of God might protect us and provide for us. (Allow a few moments to answer any questions about the activity.) Let them start. Begin timing, announcing every 60 seconds for the groups to go on to the next Commandment if they have not already done so.

As groups are working, distribute the ribbon and glue to each group. When they are finished, instruct them to make a wall-hanging with the slips of paper, ribbon, and glue, to display God's precepts—and His loving motivation to protect us and to provide for us—for the meeting room wall or door.

WORK OUT (10 minutes)

Ask: **Isn't it exciting to realize that God's purpose in giving His commands is to protect us from harm and provide good things for us? Does it motivate you? Is that why you should make right choices?** Allow time for response from students.

Ask: **Which of the following do you think is**

Matthew 22:34

a good answer to the question your Workbooks asked this past week, "Why Choose Right?" Have group members raise their hands after each statement to indicate whether they consider it a good reason to choose right.

- Because we could get in trouble with our parents if we don't

- Because choosing wrong would be a bad witness

- Because God will love us more if we choose right

- Because choosing right is safer

- Because choosing right brings God's protection and provision into our lives

- Because choosing right is just the right thing to do

- Because choosing wrong could get us mixed up in the wrong crowd

- Because of who God is

Say: **Some of those statements are not necessarily true, of course, and some of them (like "choosing right brings God's protection and provision into our lives") are certainly good things. But ultimately, we should choose right not because it benefits us, but because God is God, and He is God alone.**

Ask students to turn to page 44 in their *Right Choices* Workbooks. Have students read the statements one through six aloud and discuss the benefits listed or any other benefits of choosing the blue door.

WORD UP (15 minutes)

Enlist one or two students to write out the following verses on the chalkboard or newsprint: *2 Samuel 7:22; James 4:7.*

Say: **Many of us feel uncomfortable with God's position on various matters. Our ways are not His ways, so our tendency is to excuse and justify our way as the right way. But when we do that, we are deceived into believing that the wrong things are**

right and the right things are "not for us."

When you decide, however, to compare your attitudes and actions to God and what He says, you are acknowledging that He is God. You are agreeing with King David, who said, *"How great you are, O Sovereign Lord! There is no one like you, and there is no God but you"* (2 Sam. 7:22). You are saying that He is the Righteous Judge, that He alone defines and decides what things are right and what things are wrong. . . and He does that simply by being God. You are admitting that His nature defines right and wrong, that those actions and attitudes that are like Him are right, and those that are not like Him are wrong.

But even after admitting all that, there is one thing that yet remains for you to do, and that is not only to intellectually admit that God decides right and wrong, but to willfully submit to Him. As James said, *Submit yourselves, then, to God* (point to *Jas. 4:7* on the chalkboard or newsprint), saying that you give up your imagined "right" to decide what's right for you and decide from now on only to follow what God says is right. You surrender all decisions to Him and ask Him to help you submit every choice to Him and what He has said.

If you are willing to make that decision right now, I want you to bow your head and close your eyes, and silently repeat this prayer after me:

Lord, I need You. I acknowledge You as the Sovereign Lord and Righteous Judge. I submit to You and to Your authority. I admit that I have been directing my life and that, as a result, I have sinned against You. I thank You for forgiving my sins through Christ's death on the cross, and I invite Him to take His place on the throne of my life. Please fill me with the Holy Spirit and help me from now on, by His help, to submit every choice to You, in Jesus' name. Amen.

Take as much time as necessary to encourage students to respond; consider leading the group in a chorus, such as "Lord, Be Glorified," or in a hymn, such as "I Surrender All."

WRAP UP (5 minutes)

Say: **This coming week in your *Right Choices* Workbooks, you'll be continuing this process of submitting to God, the Righteous Judge, learning a new way of submitting your decisions to Him daily, hourly, even moment-by-moment.**

Ask for any final questions or comments.
Ask a student to close this week's session in prayer.

PLAN AHEAD (after close of session)

Evaluate today's group session and ask yourself these questions:

• What other resources did I need that would have made this session better?

• Are the students understanding the connection with the *Right Choices* Workbook and the group sessions?

• Am I beginning and ending on time? Am I covering all that I need to cover to make this a meaningful time for the students?

Prepare to call the members of the group and encourage them to stay current in their *Right Choices* Workbook and thank them for the contribution they are making to the group sessions. Ask if there is anything you can pray specifically for them.

Record date called,
the member's name,
and specific prayer requests
for each group member.

23

"You shall have no other gods before me."

"You shall not make for yourself an idol in the form of anything in heaven above or on the earth beneath or in the waters below."

"You shall not misuse the name of the Lord your God, for the Lord will not hold anyone guiltless who misuses his name."

"Remember the Sabbath day by keeping it holy."

"Honor your father and your mother, so that you may live long in the land the Lord your God is giving you."

"You shall not murder."

"You shall not commit adultery."

"You shall not steal."

"You shall not give false testimony against your neighbor."

"You shall not covet your neighbor's house. You shall not covet your neighbor's wife, or his manservant or maidservant, his ox or donkey, or anything that belongs to your neighbor."

group session 4

The Four Cs

BEFORE THE SESSION

❏ Review the learning activities for the coming week in the *Right Choices* Workbook.

❏ Read through the Session Plan, adjusting the activities according to your group's size and personality, highlighting portions you consider especially difficult or important, and making notes to personalize the Session Plan.

❏ Pray for your students. Ask God to help you accomplish the aims of the upcoming session, and to motivate and guide students as they pursue the daily sessions in the *Right Choices* Workbook.

❏ Be sure to have a chalkboard and chalk or newsprint sheets and markers available for the session.

❏ Prepare three blindfolds for the group session.

❏ Photocopy Reproducible Handout 4A ("Showdown in the OK Chorale," one copy for each student).

❏ Ask a student before the group session begins to be prepared to close in prayer.

❏ Memorize the "This Week's Verse," memory Scripture for Week 3.

SESSION OVERVIEW

- Warm-Up (10 min.)
- Look Back (10 min.)
- Work Out (20-25 min.)
- Word Up (10 min.)
- Wrap Up (5 min.)
- Plan Ahead (after the session)

THEME VERSE: Show me your ways, O Lord, teach me your paths; guide me in your truth and teach me (Ps. 25:4–5a).

SESSION PLAN

WARM-UP (10 minutes)

Welcome your students. As they are arriving, arrange three empty chairs (for the Warm-Up activity) facing the rest of the group.

Enlist a student to open today's session in prayer.

Ask for three volunteers from the group (two if your group is small). Invite the volunteers to come up to the front of the room (they should all be wearing shoes with shoestrings). Ask them to be seated on the chairs facing the rest of the group. Then blindfold them, explaining as you do:

We're going to begin our session today with a little competition. You'll be competing against the others at a task that requires dexterity and thought. There was a time in your life when you couldn't perform this complicated process, and someone else had to do it for you. But today you will not only have to do it, you'll have to do it blindfolded.

Next, untie the shoestrings of each volunteer, explaining as you do that they will be competing to see who can retie both shoes (in a full bow—no knots or half-bows) first. Inform the participants that they cannot touch their shoestrings until you say "Go."

Say: **Ready? Get set. . .Go!**

You'll have to watch the contestants closely, because they'll all perform the task very quickly. As soon as the first contestant is finished, declare a winner and remove the blindfolds. Then ask them to remain in their seats while you ask them a few questions:

Was it very hard to tie your shoes with a blindfold on?

What was the hardest part?

Do you remember how long it took you to learn to tie your shoes when you were little?

It probably took you weeks before you could tie shoestrings without any help. Why is it so easy that you can do it blindfolded now? (The answer you want is something like, "Because we've done it so many times we don't even have to think about it." If students don't give such an answer quickly, help them by asking leading questions, like, "How many times do you think you've tied your shoes in your lifetime?")

Collect blindfolds and ask volunteers to return to their seats.

LOOK BACK (10 minutes)

Say: **This past week in your** *Right Choices* **Workbooks, you were introduced to a process for discerning right and wrong, a process for making moral choices—the "4Cs." Can anyone remember what each of those four steps in decision-making are?** Give ample time and encouragement for students to recall the 4Cs—Consider the choice, Compare it to God, Commit to God's way, and Count on God's protection and provision. Ask a student to write each step on the chalkboard or newsprint as the group names each one.

Say: **But you may say to yourselves, "That all sounds okay, but who's going to stop and do all that stuff every time they face a decision? Who's going to take the time to say, 'Let's see, now, do I do this or do that? Well, first I gotta consider the choice, then I compare it to God, then I commit. . .'" And, of course, you'd be right. Nobody's going to do that. But it's like tying your shoes.**

Have students describe for the group, in simple and complete terminology, the steps for tying a shoestring. Give ample time and encouragement for students to respond. They might say, for example, "First, you take a shoestring in each hand. Then you cross them and. . ."

Ask: **Do you take time to think through each of those steps when you tie a shoestring now? Why not?**

Say: **Well, in the same way that the steps of tying shoestrings have become second nature to you now, so that you can do it with your eyes closed, the 4Cs can become second nature to you; it can become an almost automatic process for making right choices. The key, just** like it was with tying shoes, is practice.

WORK OUT (20-25 minutes)

Distribute "Showdown in the OK Chorale" (Reproducible Handout 4A). Ask students to read "Showdown in the OK Chorale" silently.

Ask: **What do you do? How would you apply the 4Cs process to this situation? What's the first step in submitting your will to God?** (Consider the choice; in other words, recognize that this is a potential choice between right and wrong.)

Say: **Okay, so you've considered the choice. You recognize this as a key decision that doesn't just involve what would be the most fun or the smartest decision, but it's also a choice between your way and God's way. What's the next step in submitting to God in this situation?** (Compare it to God)

Ask: **How do you compare it to God?** (Look at any precepts that apply, identify the principle involved, and recognize the attribute of God they point to). **So, for example, what precepts apply?** (*"You shall not give false testimony,"* Ex. 20:16; *"Do not lie,"* Lev. 19:11; *"Speak the truth to each other,"* Zech. 8:16; etc.) **What is the principle involved?** (honesty/truthfulness) **How does that relate to the person of God?** (God is true, God does not lie; therefore, lying is wrong and truthfulness is right.)

Ask: **Okay, but what about all those considerations you have to think about? You weren't really that involved; it was Bud's idea; you didn't want to do it in the first place; and you might miss the weekend youth group trip.** Try to guide students to the realization that whether or not those things are true, the choice is between committing to God's way or rejecting His way. Trying to decide yourself what is the right course of action in a situation is rejecting His way instead of simply admitting what God has said, submitting to His revelation of right and wrong, and committing yourself to following it.

Say: **So, if you progress to the third step, what would you do if you were to commit to God's way in this situation?** (Allow answers.) **Does it seem pretty clear to you?**

Ask: **What might be the results of your action? Would unpleasant consequences** result? What kinds of protection and provision might eventually (or immediately) result from your action? Should that be the reason for committing to God's way?

WORD UP (10 minutes)

Distribute Bibles to students.

Ask students to turn to *Psalm 25*. Ask a volunteer to read the following verses aloud:

Psalm 25:4-5,8-10,12-13,21

Ask: **How can the 4Cs help you to follow God's ways and be instructed in His truth?** *(v. 5)*

Does this Psalm say anything about God's motivation? *(v. 10)* **If so, what?**

According to this Psalm what kinds of protection and provision follow those who make right choices? *(vv. 13,21)* **How do those things apply to us today?**

Ask students to turn to page 60 in their Workbooks. Ask for volunteers to share their "manifesto" with the group. Be prepared to share your personal manifesto if the students ask you to do so.

WRAP UP (5 minutes)

Say: **Many choices we face in our daily lives can be as obvious or easy as "Showdown in the OK Chorale." This week in your** *Right Choices* **Workbooks, you're going to get more practice in the 4Cs, applying the process to a realistic situation.**

Ask: **Do you have any questions or comments?**

Ask a student to close this session in prayer.

PLAN AHEAD (after close of session)

Secretly enlist one student to act as your accomplice in the next session's Warm-Up activity. Provide him or her with the answers to the "Scramble to Win" game, and with instructions to study the answers in order to unscramble the words before everyone else in the group session, and then to wait until he or she suspects someone is almost finished before excitedly announcing completion of the game.

Evaluate today's group session and ask yourself these questions:

- Am I spending enough time in prayer and preparation for these sessions?

- Am I accomplishing the session aims for the sessions?

Call group members to encourage them and to thank them for their contribution they make to the group. Ask if there is anything you can pray specifically for them.

Record date called, the member's name, and specific prayer requests for each group member.

27

You're in your sixth period class, which is chorus, the "OK Chorale." You can't wait for the day to end, because you're leaving right after school for a weekend rafting trip with the church youth group.

The chorus teacher, Miss Melody, leaves for a few moments to take something to the school office. Soon after her departure, your friends Bud Smedley and Janice Porter open the classroom windows.

"I've got a great idea," Bud says. "Let's lift Miss Melody's desk and chair through the window and set it out on the lawn."

"Why would you want to do that?" you ask.

"Just for fun," Janice answers. "A harmless little prank."

"Not me," you say. "She could come back any minute."

"But we need your help," Bud begs. "We can't lift the desk all by ourselves."

You shake your head no.

"Just help us get the desk through the window," he pleads. "We'll do the rest."

You hesitate.

"Please?" Janice says.

You shrug and sigh and walk to the desk with them. Janice and Bud clear the things off the surface of the desk.

"We've gotta work quick," Bud says.

The others in the room stop talking and throwing paper wads to watch the prank take shape.

You help Bud and Janice get the desk outside. They come back; Bud grabs the chair and Janice starts to transport the pens, knickknacks, file folders and other items that had been cleared from the desk's surface. You dust your hands off.

"You guys better hurry," you say. "She could be back any time."

As if on cue, Miss Melody enters the room to catch you walking back to your seat. Bud is standing outside with the chair, and Janice is straddling the window, half in and half out, with an armload of Miss Melody's things.

Miss Melody blows her stack, and demands that everything be returned immediately to its former position. Then she turns to you. "Were you a part of this?" she asks.

You freeze. You and Miss Melody face each other like two gunfighters. You didn't want to be a part of this in the first place. And you were heading back to your seat, so it's not like you're as much to blame as Bud and Janice. Besides, the youth group is leaving right after school; if she gives a detention, you could miss the trip. What do you say?

Honest to God

SESSION AIMS

This session will:

- reinforce students' understanding of the 4Cs
- help students apply the 4C process to the issue of cheating versus honesty

BEFORE THE SESSION

❑ Review the learning activities for the coming week in the *Right Choices* Workbook.

❑ Read through the Session Plan, adjusting the activities according to your group's size and makeup.

❑ Pray for your students, asking God to keep them faithful to the group meetings and in working through the *Right Choices* Workbook.

❑ If you have not yet done so, contact one student to act as your accomplice in this week's Warm-Up activity (see instructions under Plan Ahead at the end of session 4).

❑ Photocopy Reproducible Handout 5A ("Scramble to Win") on page 32, and have enough copies and pencils for each student in the group.

❑ Have Bibles available for students to use.

❑ Memorize the "This Week's Verse," memory Scripture for Week 4.

SESSION OVERVIEW

- Warm-Up (10 min.)
- Look Back (10 min.)
- Work Out (20-25 min.)
- Word Up (10 min.)
- Wrap Up (5 min.)
- Plan Ahead (after the session)

THEME VERSE: "I know, my God, that you test the heart and are pleased with integrity" (1 Chron. 29:17a).

SESSION PLAN

WARM-UP (10 minutes)

Welcome your students and chat with them freely about the events of this week and their discoveries in the *Right Choices* Workbook.

When everyone is seated, enlist a student to open today's session in prayer.

Distribute pencils, Bibles, and Reproducible Handout 5A ("Scramble to Win") to each student. Announce that they will be competing to see who can unscramble all the words first. Explain that they may use their Bibles if they wish. When everyone is ready, give the signal to begin. Your "accomplice" should fill in the answers quickly, and then watch the others very carefully, announcing that he or she has unscrambled all the words just before the real first person to finish.

Proclaim your accomplice the winner and then ask if any others were close.

Allow time for students to practice and repeat "This Week's Verse," memory Scripture verses from memory. Encourage students to learn the verses if they have not done so.

LOOK BACK (10 minutes)

Ask: **How would you react if I told you that [your accomplice's name] cheated in the "Scramble to Win" game?** Allow students to react freely.

Say: **Of course, I gave [accomplice] the answers, and that game was no big deal, right? But what if [accomplice] had done it alone? Would that have been wrong?** Allow some response, but try to postpone reference to the 4Cs until the "Work Out" portion.

Ask: **What if he or she had cheated you out of an expensive prize? Would that change things?** Allow students to respond, and then follow up by asking, **Would it spoil the game for you? Would**

it make you mad? Would it affect your opinion of [accomplice]?

Have students share what they learned from this past week's assignments. Allow several students to recount the purpose of the *Right Choices* Workbook sessions. Have them share the new insights that they have learned from the Workbook. Ask if any are struggling with anything that they have read or heard during the *Right Choices* course? Allow several students to share their discoveries and insights, and address any questions or struggles they may have.

WORK OUT (20 minutes)

Divide students into two groups. Give a Bible, marker, and newsprint (or chalk and chalkboard) to each group.

Instruct Group A to brainstorm through a discussion of whether or not cheating—on a school test, in an election, in a game—is wrong. Remind them to use what they've learned of the 4C process in their *Right Choices* Workbooks. They may also refer to the Bible references used in the "Scramble to Win" game. They may wish to list the first three "Cs" on the newsprint to use as an outline. Inform them that they will need to appoint a "reporter" to relate their discoveries to the entire group after 10 minutes. If necessary, as they are working, be available to remind them of the "Precept–Principle–Person" method for discerning truth.

Instruct Group B to brainstorm ways in which God's standard of honesty and trustworthiness—which forbids cheating and other forms of dishonesty—protects and provides for them. Ask them to list their ideas on the newsprint under "provide" and "protect." Encourage them to become as specific as possible. They, too, may refer to the Bible references used in the "Scramble to Win" game. Inform them that someone in their group will also need to report to the entire group after 10 minutes.

After 10 minutes of work, bring both groups together. Ask Group A to report on their conclusions about cheating—if cheating is wrong and, if so, why? Next ask Group B to report on ways that we can count on God's protection and provision if we conform to His standard of honesty and integrity.

Have students turn to page 80 in their Workbooks. Ask several to share what ending they

wrote for Dan's story. Praise and encourage them for their efforts. Ask volunteers to describe a situation in their life that would have ended differently if they had committed to God's way.

WORD UP (10 minutes)

Instruct the group to open their Bibles to *1 Chronicles 29:17*. Ask a volunteer to read it aloud.

Ask: **What do you think it means that He tests our hearts?** Allow students to offer their ideas freely, without pronouncing any right or wrong. Guide them to realize that God tests our hearts mainly by seeing how we respond to opportunities to make choices.

Define *integrity* for the students. Ask: **What do you think that verse means by "integrity?"** Allow students to offer their opinions freely.

Ask: **Why do you think integrity pleases God?** Allow as many students as possible to respond, guiding them by your responses to recall the "Precept–Principle–Person" formula, perhaps saying:

God forbids dishonest gain and cheating (precept)
   because He values honesty (principle),
   and He values honesty
   because He is true and trustworthy (person). **That is why cheating is wrong, and that is also why we do ourselves a favor when we conform to His absolute standard, because we can then benefit from His protection and provision.**

WRAP UP (5 minutes)

Ask several students in rapid succession, **Is cheating wrong? Why?**

Ask several students in rapid succession, **How might God's standard of honesty provide for you and protect you?**

Ask: **Do you have any final questions or comments?**

Ask a student to close this week's session in prayer.

PLAN AHEAD (after close of session)

Ask three groups of two students each to perform role plays (Reproducible Handout 6A, p. 35) to begin the next session. (If you have a small group, enlist just two students to perform all three role plays.)

Evaluate today's group session and ask yourself these questions:

• What other resources did I need that would have made this session better?

• Are the students understanding the connection with the *Right Choices* Workbook and the group sessions?

• Am I beginning and ending on time? Am I covering all that I need to cover to make this a meaningful time for the students?

Prepare to call the members of the group and encourage them to stay current in their *Right Choices* Workbook and thank them for the contribution they are making to the group sessions. Ask if there is anything you can pray specifically for them.

Answers to Reproducible Handout 5A("Scramble to Win").
Scripture are from NIV.
1. honest, 2. dishonest, 3. integrity, 4. kiss, 5. truthful,
6. scales, 7. ephah, 8. bath, 9. uprightness, 10. integrity,
11. duplicity, 12. securely, 13. righteousness, 14. wickedness,
15. weights, 16. measures

Record date called,
the member's name,
and specific prayer requests
for each group member.

31

1. _____

2. _____

3. _____

4. _____

5. _____

6. _____

7. _____

8. _____

9. _____

10. _____

11. _____

12. _____

13. _____

14. _____

15. _____

16. _____

"Use **shento**[1] scales and honest weights, an honest ephah and an honest hin. I am the Lord your God, who brought you out of Egypt" (Lev. 19:36).

Deacons, likewise, are to be men worthy of respect, sincere, not indulging in much wine, and not pursuing **ethnodiss**[2] gain (1 Tim. 3:8).

"I know, my God, that you test the heart and are pleased with **yettirgin**[3]" (1 Chron. 29:17a).

An honest answer is like a **skis**[4] on the lips (Prov. 24:26).

A **thufturl**[5] witness gives honest testimony, but a false witness tells lies (Prov. 12:17).

"You are to use accurate **alcess**,[6] an accurate **hepah**[7] and an accurate **thab**[8]" (Ezek. 45:10).

May integrity and **pressunight**[9] protect me, because my hope is in you (Ps. 25:21).

The **grintitey**[10] of the upright guides them, but the unfaithful are destroyed by their **clidupity**[11] (Prov. 11:3).

The man of integrity walks **curselye**,[12] but he who takes crooked paths will be found out (Prov. 10:9).

Sournightesse[13] guards the man of integrity, but **swindeckes**[14] overthrows the sinner (Prov. 13:6).

You must have accurate and honest **thewigs**[15] and **seaserum**,[16] so that you may live long in the land the Lord your God is giving you (Deut. 25:15).

What the World Needs Now

SESSION AIMS

This session will:

• reinforce students' understanding of the 4Cs

• help students apply the 4C process to the issue of mistreatment versus love

BEFORE THE SESSION

❏ Review the learning activities for the coming week in the *Right Choices* Workbook.

❏ Read through the Session Plan, adjusting the activities according to your group's size and makeup.

❏ Pray for your students, asking God to use the group meetings and *Right Choices* Workbook to guide each student to a biblical, godly method for making right choices.

❏ Photocopy Reproducible Handout 6A ("Three Role Plays," p. 35) and cut along dotted lines to distribute to participants in the role plays in the Warm-Up period of this session.

❏ Cover large section of one wall with newsprint or table paper for a "Graffiti Wall" for the Work Out period of this session. Obtain a collection of colored markers or chalk.

❏ Have Bibles available for students to use.

❏ Memorize the "This Week's Verse," memory Scripture for Week 5.

SESSION OVERVIEW

• Warm-Up (15 min.)
• Look Back (15 min.)
• Work Out (15 min.)
• Word Up (10 min.)
• Wrap Up (5 min.)
• Plan Ahead (after the session)

THEME VERSE: This is the message you heard from the beginning: We should love one another (1 John 3:11).

SESSION PLAN

WARM-UP (15 minutes)

Welcome your students and chat with them freely about the events of this week and their discoveries in the *Right Choices* Workbook.

When everyone is seated, enlist a student to open today's session in prayer.

If you have not done so already, enlist three groups (of two students each) to perform role plays to begin today's session (if you have a small group, enlist just two students to perform all three role plays). Distribute the role plays from Reproducible Handout 6A ("Three Role Plays") among the three groups and have them present each in turn.

Allow students time to practice and repeat "This Week's Verse" memory Scripture from memory. Encourage students to learn the verse for Week 5.

LOOK BACK (15 minutes)

Remind students that two weeks ago in our Workbook, we worked through the 4Cs process for making right choices in relation to cheating and dishonesty. Ask, **What was the focus of this past week's studies in the Workbook?** (Love.) Ask: **How do you think the three role plays we've just seen relate to that subject?** Allow responses.

Say: **Someone describe what was happening in the first role play.** Allow a student—one of the actors if necessary—to offer a synopsis of the first role play. Ask: **What was wrong with [bigoted actor's] action?** (Allow response.) **How do you know it was wrong?** Encourage students here to talk through the 4C process, applying it to the first role play.

Say: **Someone describe what went on in the second role play.** Allow a student—an actor if necessary—to offer a synopsis of the role play. Ask: **Do you think the jealous actor's behavior was wrong?** Ask: **How do you know it was wrong?** Encourage them to apply the 4C process to the second role play.

Say: **Someone describe the third role play.** Allow a student—an actor if necessary—to offer a synopsis of the role play. Ask: **What was wrong with [verbally abusive actor's] action?** (Allow response) **How do you know it was wrong?** Encourage students to talk through the 4C process, applying it to the third role play.

WORK OUT (15 minutes)

Distribute colored markers or chalk to each student.

Direct students to the newsprint or table paper that you have prepared as a "Graffiti Wall."

Say: **For the next 10 minutes, we're going to create a "Graffiti Wall." Allow your creativity to run wild. Each of you write or draw your definition of love. You can write a sentence beginning, "Love is. . ." You can begin your definition with the words, "Love means. . ." or draw a picture or a symbol to represent love. Or you can do all three. Whatever you do, make it as complete a definition as you can, and as creative and interesting as you can.**

Allow students to work. Encourage a high-energy, time-efficient approach. Circulate among the students as they work, commenting on their definitions or representations of love. Make this an activity that prompts them to contemplate the basis of their definitions.

WORD UP (10 minutes)

When the "Graffiti Wall" is complete, ask students to return to their seats and open their Bibles to *Ephesians 5*.

Say: **It looks like we've discovered many different ways to define and express love. And those definitions come from a lot of different places.**

Ask several different people: **Where did you learn your definition of love? Where did it come from?** Explain that they will discover a biblical definition of love. Ask a student to read *Ephesians 5:25-29*. Restate that *verses 28* and *29*, *"Husbands ought to love their wives as their own bodies. . . After all, no one ever hated his own body, but he feeds and cares for it."* Say: **According to God's Word, to love someone means to value their happiness, health, and spiritual growth as much as you do your own. If that's what love really is, then what does that say about some of the things we call love?** Allow responses.

Ask: **If that's the kind of love God commands—if that's the kind of love He values, and the kind of love He is—how should submitting and committing to Him through the 4Cs process change the way we live?** Allow students to respond, encouraging them to offer specific, real-life examples.

Ask students to turn to page 99 in their Workbooks. Allow volunteers to read the finishing touches they wrote for Monica's story. Discuss the endings as a group

without putting down individuals for their efforts.

WRAP UP (5 minutes)

Ask several students, **Is abuse, jealousy, and bigotry wrong? Why?** Ask several students, **How might God's standard of love provide for you and protect you?** Ask: **Do you have any questions or comments?** Ask a student to close this week's session in prayer.

PLAN AHEAD (after close of session)

Session 7 calls for six tools or utensils. If six of the listed or similar items (read Group Session 7's "Warm-Up" activity, p. 36) are not easily obtainable, plan now to borrow or collect such items.

Evaluate today's group session and ask yourself these questions:

* What other resources did I need to make this session better?

* Are the students understanding the connection with the Workbook and the group sessions?

* Am I beginning and ending on time? Am I covering all that I need to cover to make this a meaningful time for the students?

Call group members and encourage them to stay current in their Workbooks. Thank them for the contribution they make to the group sessions. Ask if there is anything you can pray specifically for them.

> **Record date called, the member's name, and specific prayer requests for each group member.**

Reproducible Handout 6A

Three Role Plays

··

INSTRUCTIONS FOR ACTORS: Take a few moments to plan your role play together, deciding who will play each role, and how you will act out the scene below. Try to create an appropriate ending for your scene: clever, funny, or challenging.

One of you is a new kid at school, asking directions to Mrs. Dillpickle's study hall; the other must portray a person who clearly doesn't like the new kid because of his or her race/hair color/eye color/accent/clothes (pick one). The new kid should respond patiently and respectfully to the other person's prejudice.

··

INSTRUCTIONS FOR ACTORS: Take a few moments to plan your role play together, deciding who will play each role, and how you will act out the scene below. Try to create an appropriate ending for your scene: clever, funny, or challenging.

The two of you are talking about Tracy Prepster, one of the most popular kids at school, who also goes to church with both of you. One of you is extremely jealous; the other is proud that a kid from your church is so successful and popular in such a large school.

··

INSTRUCTIONS FOR ACTORS: Take a few moments to plan your role play together, deciding who will play each role, and how you will act out the scene below. Try to create an appropriate ending for your scene: clever, funny, or challenging.

One of you is making fun of Fat Linda, who has been the subject of much abuse since third grade. The other expresses discomfort—and regret—over the way Linda is so often treated.

··

35

group session 7

Sweet Chastity

SESSION AIMS

This session will:

- reinforce students' understanding of the 4Cs
- help students apply the 4C process to the issue of sex

BEFORE THE SESSION

❑ Review the learning activities for the coming week in the *Right Choices* Workbook.

❑ Read through the Session Plan. Adjust activities to fit your group's size and makeup.

❑ Pray for your students, asking God to help them truly confront their own struggles regarding romance and sexuality.

❑ Obtain at least six of the following household tools or utensils for the Warm-Up activity, "Name That Tool": T square, whisk (egg beater), muffin separator, light timer, Allen wrench, plunger, voltage meter, meat tenderizer, egg separator, ball peen hammer, noodle maker, turkey baster, leather punch, tin snips, egg slicer, cookie dough scoop, sock sorter.

❑ Have a chalkboard and chalk or newsprint sheets and markers available for the session.

❑ Photocopy Reproducible Handout 7A ("Choice Moments") and cut the page along dotted lines to use during this session's Work Out activity.

❑ Have Bibles available for students to use.

❑ Memorize the "This Week's Verse," memory Scripture for Week 6.

SESSION OVERVIEW

- Warm-Up (15 min.)
- Look Back (10 min.)
- Word Up (10 min.)
- Work Out (20 min.)
- Wrap Up (5 min.)
- Plan Ahead (after the session)

SESSION PLAN

WARM-UP (15 minutes)

Welcome your students; encourage them to talk about their discoveries in the *Right Choices* Workbook. Remind them that the coming week is the last in the *Right Choices* Workbook.

When everyone is seated, enlist a student to open today's session in prayer.

Ask for three volunteers to play "Name That Tool." Line the volunteers up behind a table and place two of the following objects on the table in front of each of them (for a total of six objects).

T square	whisk (egg beater)
muffin separator	light timer
Allen wrench	plunger
voltage meter	meat tenderizer
egg separator	ball peen hammer
noodle maker	turkey baster
leather punch	tin snips
egg slicer	cookie dough scoop
sock sorter	

Here are the rules: Explain that as a group you're going to play "Name That Tool." Each of our three contestants has two household tools or kitchen utensils on the table in front of them. Their job is to explain, briefly and believably, the purpose of the tool. They may choose to explain the true purpose of the tool, OR (even if they know the true purpose), they may make up a fictional explanation of what it does.

They score points in two ways: One point for every person who believes a true definition of the tool's purpose, and two points for every person who believes a made-up definition of the tool's purpose.

In round one, each contestant will choose one of the tools in front of him or her and then offer an explanation of what the tool is for. Then ask how many in the "studio audience" think he or she has given the true definition of the tool's purpose. If the definition was the true definition, that contestant will score one point for everyone in the audience who agreed with the definition. If it was a fictional definition, the contestant will score two points for everyone in the audience who agreed with the definition. The score will be recorded on the chalkboard (or newsprint), and it will be the next contestant's turn, followed, of course, by the final contestant.

Round two will be identical, except in the reverse order. The contestants, If they know the true purpose of the tool, must decide whether to try for the lower or higher scoring opportunity. If they don't know the true purpose of the tool, of course, they must try to bluff the audience.

Ask if everyone understands the rules. After questions are answered play "Name That Tool!"

Allow the three volunteers to play the game as you've outlined it while you or another student volunteer tallies the score on the chalkboard or newsprint.

After both rounds of the game have been played, declare a winner, thank all contestants, and allow them to return to their seats.

Allow time for students to practice and repeat "This Week's Verse," memory Scripture verse from memory. Encourage students to learn the memory verses if they have not done so.

LOOK BACK (10 minutes)

Ask the three contestants: **Did you know what your objects were? Did you know what all the tools were for? Was it hard to think up fictional uses for any of the tools? What do you think would happen if you tried to use an egg beater to flip pancakes? What would happen if you tried to use a plunger to tune your car engine?** Let students explore the imaginary results of such silly scenarios.

Ask: **Why wouldn't those tools work in those cases?** Because that's not the purpose for which they were intended.

Ask: **Now, someone may ask, "What does all this have to do with the subject of this past week's daily studies?" Any ideas?**

WORD UP (10 minutes)

Ask a volunteer to record key words and phrases on the chalkboard or newsprint as you indicate (these phrases are indicated below with an *).

Say: **Just like the person who designed the Allen wrench intended it for a specific purpose, and just like an egg slicer isn't much good for chopping wood, so sex was created to be used in a specific way. It was designed to be:**

* between a man and a woman. Ask a student to read *Genesis 2:18,21-22.*

* between a husband and wife. Ask a student to read *Genesis 13:4. 2:23,24*
Heb. 13:4

Say: **Marriage was also designed for specific purposes; it was designed to be used for:**

* procreation (having children). Ask a student to read *Genesis 1:28.*

* spiritual unity and true emotional intimacy. Ask another student to read *Genesis 2:24.*

Ask: **What can happen when sex is used for a purpose other than that for which God designed it?** Allow students to offer their input, guiding them to identify such things as broken relationships, STDs, unwanted pregnancies and abortion, the loss of trust in relationships, etc.

WORK OUT (20 minutes)

Say: **We've had six weeks of exposure to the 4C process for making right choices. Can anyone write those four steps on the chalkboard (or newsprint) for me?** Allow a volunteer to write the 4Cs onto the chalkboard or newsprint while you pass out the slips of paper you've prepared from the Reproducible Handout 7A ("Choice Moments").

Explain that for the next few moments, you're going to try to help the students apply the 4C process to three different situations. Three students will read a situation from a slip of paper you've prepared; and then say, **All of us will work together to see how the 4Cs process for making right choices might possibly apply to these situations.**

Ask the student with "Choice Moment" #1 to read the situation, then ask all students the following questions:

• **How would you apply the 4Cs process to this situation?**

• **What would it mean to "Consider the Choice?"** It would mean evaluating the situation and recognizing that it represents a choice, not between matters of taste, nor even between what I think is right or wrong, but a choice between what is right or wrong—objectively.

• **How would I compare it to God?** Using the Precept—Principle—Person process; see Workbook pp. 111—113 for one possible approach.

• **What would it mean in this situation to commit to God's way?**

• **What would counting on God's provision and protection involve?**

Repeat those questions for each of the three situations, urging students to thoroughly and candidly work through the 4C process.

WRAP UP (5 minutes)

Ask several students in rapid succession, **Is premarital sex or extramarital sex wrong? Why?**

Ask several students in rapid succession, **How might God's standards for sex provide for you and protect you?**

Ask students to turn to page 104 in their Workbooks. Enlist someone to read aloud "This Week's Verse," and then to lead in a group reading of the verse. Have students turn to page 120 and write the verse in the margin by the prayer. Ask a youth to explain what *1 Corinthians 6:20* says about God's standard for sex.

Ask: **Do you have any questions or comments?**

Ask a student to close this week's session in prayer.

PLAN AHEAD (after close of session)

Evaluate today's group session and ask yourself these questions:

• Are the students understanding the connection with the *Right Choices* Workbook and the group sessions?

• Am I beginning and ending on time? Am I covering all that I need to cover to make this a meaningful time for the students?

Prepare to call the members of the group and encourage them to stay current in their *Right Choices* Workbook and thank them for the contribution they are making to the group sessions. Ask if there is anything you can pray specifically for them.

Record date called, the member's name, and specific prayer requests for each group member.

38

. . . .

#1

"My boyfriend and I just had an argument. He wants to do more than just kiss on dates, and I'm afraid if I don't let him have his way, I'll lose him. In fact, he told me that there are plenty of girls who will let boys do what he wants to do. I think I really love him, so it wouldn't be so bad, would it?"

. . . .

#2

Kerri and I are having a great time hanging out together. She's a really nice girl and we have known each other for a long time. We even went to the same elementary school together. I never thought of her as the "girlfriend" type. But man, last night was really weird. She and I were just hanging out at her house and we started kissing and then things started to get out of control. I finally stopped it before we went too far. We are really not interested in a relationship, we just are really curious about sex. As long as we are careful and just experiment with each other, there can't be any harm in that, can there?

. . . .

#3

"We get FAO—the cable channel For Adults Only—and sometimes when my parents aren't home, I'll watch it. I figure there's nothing wrong with it. After all, I'm still a virgin and everything, I'm just watching stuff."

. . . .

group
session

Welcome
to the Next Level

SESSION AIMS

This session will:

- challenge students to take a Daniel-like stand for truth in a Babylonian-type culture
- plan with students how to share the message of truth
- conclude the *Right Choices* Workbook study and group sessions

BEFORE THE SESSION

❑ Obtain *Setting Youth Free to Make Right Choices* Five-part Video Series to use as a follow through to this Workbook study.

❑ Read through the Session Plan. Adjust activities to fit your group's size and makeup.

❑ Pray for your students, asking God to strengthen them and embolden them to take a stand for truth.

❑ Be sure to have a chalkboard and chalk or newsprint sheets and markers available.

❑ Photocopy Reproducible Handout 8A ("Two Role Plays") one copy for each actor.

❑ Photocopy Reproducible Handout 8B ("My View of Truth") one copy for each student. Be sure to have a pen and/or pencil for everyone in the class, too.

❑ Have Bibles available for students to use.

❑ Memorize the "This Week's Verse," memory Scripture for Week 7.

SESSION OVERVIEW

- Warm-Up (15 min.)
- Look Back (10 min.)
- Word Up (10 min.)
- Work Out (20 min.)
- Wrap Up (5 min.)
- Plan Ahead (after the session)

THEME VERSE: God. . . wants all men to be saved and to come to a knowledge of the truth (1 Tim. 2:4).

SESSION PLAN

WARM-UP (15 minutes)

Welcome your students, eliciting from them any comments or questions about the past week's discoveries in the *Right Choices* Workbook.

When everyone is seated, enlist a student to open today's session in prayer.

If you have not done so already, enlist two groups (of three students each) to perform role plays to begin today's session. If you have a small group, enlist just one group to perform both role plays. Distribute the role plays from Reproducible Handout 8A ("Two Role Plays") among the groups.

Allow time for students to practice and repeat "This Week's Verse," memory Scripture verses. Encourage students to learn all of the memory verses if they have not done so.

Say: **We're going to begin our last *Right Choices* session together with two brief role plays, portraying two different versions of an event in the life of Daniel. One role play will depict the way things really happened, and the other will show the way things might have happened if Daniel had acted differently.**

LOOK BACK (15 minutes)

Thank role-play participants and allow them to take their seats with the rest of the group.

Ask the following questions and allow youth to respond: **What was different about the two role plays? Which role play reflected the way things really happened, according to the Bible? Why did the second role play end differently than the first? Can you think of other possible endings to the second role play? What do you think is the point of the two role plays? What can we learn from them? How do they apply to us?**

WORD UP (15 minutes)

Say: **Have you ever made a wish on a star, or before blowing out birthday candles, or before throwing a penny into a wishing well? Can someone share a wish that you remember making?** Allow several group members to tell the story of a wish that they made.

Do you know that God has "wishes," too? What do you think God wishes for? Allow several group members to offer ideas.

First Timothy 2 is where you'll find out one of God's "wishes." Look at *verse 4*, which says that God wants all men to be saved and to come to a knowledge of the truth. What do you think that means? Can anyone put that "wish" in other words?** Allow several group members to offer their own paraphrase of that verse.

Do you realize that we can help make God's wish come true? We can. How do you think we can do that? Allow several group members to offer ideas. Ask, **Does Daniel's story suggest an answer to us?**

Summarize the fact that we can help men and women to be saved and to come to a knowledge of the truth as we take a Daniel-like stand in our Babylonian-type culture. We can help God's wish come true by fearlessly and confidently "telling the truth." Emphasize that we can tell what we know about absolute truth; what we've learned about right and wrong and Who determines it; and what we've discovered about making good choices in a world gone bad. We can tell our friends, families, churches, and communities.

Ask: **From what you've learned in your *Right Choices* Workbooks this past week, what do you think it means to take a "Daniel-like" stand for truth?** Allow several group members to offer ideas.

Ask: **What are some ways that you plan to stand for truth in the future? How?** Allow several group members to offer ideas.

Ask: **What if someone accuses you of being intolerant? What if your stand for truth gets you into trouble or makes someone mad at you? How will you respond?** Allow several group members to offer ideas.

Ask students to turn to page 134 in their Workbooks. Ask them to review their guidelines they wrote under "Your Standard for Truth." Discuss the question on page 134, "Do you think that kind of behavior will guarantee that you'll never be criticized or accused of being intolerant?"

WORK OUT (15 minutes)

Say: **We've learned a lot these past few weeks, as we've discovered a whole new way of making choices, a whole new way of looking at truth and a whole new way of looking at God's Law. What has been the most exciting or life-changing discovery you've made these past seven weeks?** Allow several group members to respond.

Distribute Reproducible Handout 8B ("My View of Truth") to each student. Make sure each has a pen or pencil to complete the brief survey students initially confronted in Week 1 of their *Right Choices* Workbooks.

Say: **This handout** (referring to Reproducible Handout 8B "My View of Truth") **contains seven statements that you were asked to respond to in our first week of *Right Choices* Workbook study. I want you to read through this brief survey again, answering each statement according to your present view of truth. . . be honest, and respond to each statement according to what you believe today.** Allow students time to thoughtfully complete "My View of Truth." When they are all finished, continue the session.

Ask: **Did any of you respond differently to these statements than you did seven weeks ago? How were your answers different?** Allow several students to explain their answers.

Ask: **Why did you answer differently this time. . . because you knew which answers were "right," or because you've changed some of your beliefs about truth?**

Say: **We have learned some great truths in the past few weeks of study. It would be a great mistake on our part if we did not share what we have learned. Think of three people that you know who could benefit from knowing the 4Cs process of making right decisions.** Brainstorm some ways that they could involve their friends in the Workbook study or the Video Series. If they are unfamiliar with the Video Series, tell them about it (using the copy from the introduction of the Leader's Guide or by showing the promotion video of *Setting Youth Free to Make Right Choices* Video

Series) and ask the students to commit to bringing a friend with them to the five-part Video Series.

WRAP UP (5 minutes)

Say: **We're going to close our final Right Choices group session with a period of prayer. I'd like us to form a circle, and join hands, and then I'd like us each to offer a prayer to God, perhaps thanking Him for what we've learned, maybe asking Him to help us make right choices in a specific area, and asking Him for the strength and wisdom to stand like Daniel in a world like ours. Let's all bow our heads, close our eyes, and pray.**

PLAN AHEAD (after close of session)

It may seem rather odd to talk about planning ahead here since the Workbook study is complete. You will remember from the introduction that the Workbook is just one phase of the Right from Wrong Campaign for Junior and Senior High Students. *Setting Youth Free to Make Right Choices* Video Series is the other track that can be taken. You may have entered the Right from Wrong Campaign through that Video Series, but if you began in the Workbook study then a whole new world awaits you. Those students who have completed the Workbook should be ready to reach out to others to share with their friends the truths that they have found in *Setting You Free to Make Right Choices Workbook.* The Video Series is fast-paced, highly motivational and will challenge your entire youth group, including the fun-seekers. The commitment level is less demanding and is a great tool to introduce the youth group to the concepts of making right choices based upon an absolute standard of truth. At the conclusion of the Video Series, begin a new group going through the *Setting You Free to Make Right Choices Workbook.*

It is important to remember that this Workbook study and Video Series can be very important resources for any new youth that may come into the group either by moving up from a lower grade level into the youth area or any who may be new Christians or new members in your church. Do not think of this Workbook study and Video Series as a one-shot offering. The 4Cs process of making good decisions is one that all students need to be made aware of.

Record prayer requests.
Also use this space to record any ideas or supplies you need
to begin the next Right Choices Workbook study or Video Series.

Two Role Plays

#1

INSTRUCTIONS FOR ACTORS: Take a few moments to plan your role play together, deciding who will play each role, and how you will act out the scene below. Your role play is based on Daniel 6. Read chapter 6 and then perform the following role play:

One of you is Daniel, the Hebrew refugee who has risen to a high position in the Babylonian government. Another is one of the Babylonian officials who discovers Daniel praying and reports him to the king. The third actor is the king.

PERFORM THE FIRST ROLE PLAY AS IT OCCURRED IN THE BIBLE. THE ACTOR PORTRAYING DANIEL MUST BE SURE TO RESPOND TO THE CHARGES AND CONSEQUENCES OF HIS ACTION WITH DIGNITY, CONFIDENCE, AND RESPECT.

#2

INSTRUCTIONS FOR ACTORS: Take a few moments to plan your role play together, deciding who will play each role, and how you will act out the scene below. Your role play is based on Daniel 6. Read chapter 6 and then perform the following role play. Try to create an appropriate ending for your scene: clever, funny, or challenging.

One of you is Daniel, the Hebrew refugee who has risen to a high position in the Babylonian government. Another is one of the Babylonian officials who discovers Daniel praying and reports him to the king. The third actor is the king.

PERFORM THIS ROLE PLAY AS IT OCCURS IN THE BIBLE, EXCEPT THAT THE ACTOR PORTRAYING DANIEL MUST RESPOND TO THE CHARGES AND CONSEQUENCES OF HIS ACTION WITH AN OBNOXIOUS, RUDE, AND ANGRY ATTITUDE. THE ENDING SHOULD ANSWER THE QUESTION, "HOW MIGHT DANIEL'S STORY HAVE ENDED DIFFERENTLY IF HE HAD NOT ACTED RIGHTEOUSLY?"

Reproducible Handout 8B

My view of Truth

What is your present "truth view"? To help you answer that question, simply mark one answer to indicate whether you agree, disagree, or are not sure about how you respond to that statement.

	agree?		
Statement	**Yes**	**No**	**Not Sure**
1. There is no such thing as "absolute truth"; people may define truth in contradictory ways and still be correct.	—	—	——
2. Everything in life is negotiable.	—	—	——
3. Only the Bible provides a clear and indisputable description of moral truth.	—	—	——
4. Nothing can be known for certain except the things you experience in your life.	—	—	——
5. When it comes to matters of morals and ethics, truth means different things to different people; no one can be sure they have the truth.	—	—	——
6. What is right for one person in a given situation might not be right for another person who encounters that same situation.	—	—	——
7. God may know the meaning of truth, but humans are not capable of grasping that knowledge.	—	—	——

Scoring Yourself

Grade yourself by circling the point value below that corresponds to each of your answers above:

Question If you scored. . .	Yes	No	Not Sure
1.	0	1	0
2.	0	1	0
3.	1	0	0
4.	0	1	0
5.	0	1	0
6.	0	1	0
7.	0	1	0

0-2 points. Uh oh. . .haven't you been listening the past seven weeks?

3-4 points. Did you do the *Right Choices* Workbook, or just attend the group sessions?

5-6 points. You're apparently coming to a knowledge of the truth.

7 points. You apparently have a strong, cohesive view of truth.

Passing on the Truth to Our Next Generation

The "Right From Wrong" message, available in numerous formats, provides a blueprint for countering the culture and rebuilding the crumbling foundations of our families.

Read It and Embrace a New Way of Thinking

The Right From Wrong Book to Adults

Right From Wrong - What You Need to Know to Help Youth Make Right Choices
by Josh McDowell & Bob Hostetler

Our youth no longer live in a culture that teaches an objective standard of right and wrong. Truth has become a matter of taste. Morality has been replaced by individual preference. And today's youth have been affected. Fifty-seven percent (57%) of our churched youth cannot state that an objective standard of right and wrong even exists!

As the centerpiece of the "Right From Wrong" Campaign, this life-changing book provides you with a biblical, yet practical, blueprint for passing on core Christian values to the next generation.

Right From Wrong, Trade Paper Book
ISBN 0-8499-3604-7

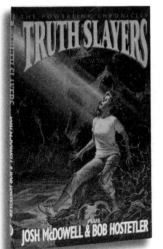

The Truth Slayers Book to Youth

The Truth Slayers - The Battle of Right From Wrong
by Josh McDowell & Bob Hostetler

This book—directed to youth—is written in the popular NovelPlus format and combines the fascinating story of Brittney Marsh, Philip Milford and Jason Withers and the consequences of their wrong choices with Josh McDowell's insights for young adults in sections called "The Inside Story."

The Truth Slayers conveys the critical "Right From Wrong" message that challenges you to rely on God's word as the absolute standard of truth in making right choices.

The Truth Slayers, Trade Paper Book
ISBN 0-8499-3662-4

Hear It and Adopt a New Way of Teaching

Right From Wrong Audio for Adults
by Josh McDowell

What is truth? In three powerful and persuasive talks based on the book *Right From Wrong*, Josh McDowell provides you, your family, and the church with a sound, thorough, biblical, and workable method to clearly understand and defend the truth. Josh explains how to identify absolutes and shows you how to teach youth to determine what is absolutely right from wrong.

Right From Wrong, Audio—104 min.
ISBN 0-8499-6195-5

See It and Commit to a New Way of Living

Truth Matters, Adult Video Series
ISBN 0-8499-8587-0

Video Series to Adults

Truth Matters for You and Tomorrow's Generation
Five-part Video Series featuring Josh McDowell

Josh McDowell is at his best in this hard-hitting series that goes beyond surface answers and quick fixes to tackle the real crisis of truth. You will discover the reason for this crisis, and more importantly, how to get you and your family back on track. This series is directed to the entire adult community and is excellent for building momentum in your church to address the loss of values within the family.

This series includes five video sessions, a comprehensive Leader's Guide including samplers from the five "Right From Wrong" Workbooks, the *Right From Wrong* book, the *Truth Slayers* book, and a 12-minute promotional video tape to motivate adults to go through the series.

Video Series to Youth

Setting You Free to Make Right Choices
Five-part Video Series featuring Josh McDowell

Through captivating video illustrations, dynamic teaching sessions, and creative group interaction, this series presents students with convincing evidence that right moral choices must be based on a standard outside of themselves. This powerful course equips your students with the understanding of what is right from what is wrong.

The series includes five video sessions, Leader's Guide with reproducible handout including samplers from the five "Right From Wrong" Workbooks, and the *Truth Slayers* book.

Setting You Free to Make
Right Choices, Youth Video Series
ISBN 0-8499-8585-4

CAMPAIGN RIGHT FROM WRONG RESOURCES

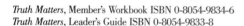

Practice It and Make Living the Truth a Habit

Workbook for Adults

Truth Matters for You and Tomorrow's Generation
Workbook by Josh McDowell with Leader's Guide

The "Truth Matters" Workbook includes 35 daily activities that help you to instill within your children and youth such biblical values as honesty, love, and sexual purity. By taking just 25 - 30 minutes each day, you will discover a fresh and effective way to teach your family how to make right choices–even in tough situations.

The "Truth Matters" Workbook is designed to be used in eight adult group sessions that encourage interaction and support building. The five daily activities between each group meeting will help you and your family make right choices a habit.

Truth Matters, Member's Workbook ISBN 0-8054-9834-6
Truth Matters, Leader's Guide ISBN 0-8054-9833-8

Workbook for College Students

Out of the Moral Maze
by Josh McDowell with Leader's Instructions

Students entering college face a culture that has lost its belief in absolutes. In today's society, truth is a matter of taste; morality of individual preference. "Out of the Moral Maze" will provide any truth-seeking collegiate with a sound moral guidance system based on God and His Word as the determining factor for making right moral choices.

Out of the Moral Maze, Member's Workbook with
Leader's Instructions
ISBN 0-8054-9832-X

Workbook for Junior High and High School Students

Setting You Free to Make Right Choices
by Josh McDowell with Leader's Guide

With a Bible-based emphasis, this Workbook creatively and systematically teaches your students how to determine right from wrong in their everyday lives–specifically applying the decision-making process to moral questions about lying, cheating, getting even, and premarital sex.

Through eight youth group meetings followed each week with five daily exercises of 20-25 minutes per day, your teenagers will be challenged to develop a life-long habit of making right moral choices.

Setting You Free to Make Right Choices, Member's Workbook
ISBN 0-8054-9828-1
Setting You Free to Make Right Choices, Leader's Guide
ISBN 0-8054-9829-X

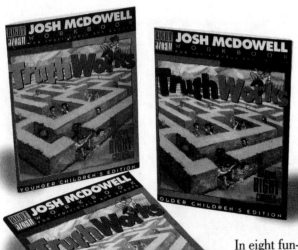

Workbook for Children

Truth Works - Making Right Choices
by Josh McDowell with Leader's Guide

To pass on the truth and reclaim a generation, we must teach God's truth when our children's minds and hearts are young and pliable. Creatively developed, "Truth Works" is two workbooks, one directed to younger children grades 1 - 3 and one to older children grades 4 - 6.

In eight fun-filled group sessions, your children will discover why such truths as honesty, justice, love, purity, self-control, mercy, and respect work to their best interests and how four simple steps will help them to make right moral choices an everyday habit.

Truth Works, Younger Children's Workbook ISBN 0-8054-9831-1
Truth Works, Older Children's Workbook ISBN 0-8054-9830-3
Truth Works, Leader's Guide ISBN 0-8054-9827-3

Contact your Christian supplier to help you obtain these "Right From Wrong" resources
and begin to make it right in your home, your church, and your community.